TRACING LOST RAILWAYS

Trevor Yorke

SHIRE PUBLICATIONS

Bloomsbury Publishing Plc

PO Box 883, Oxford, OX1 9PL, UK

1385 Broadway, 5th Floor, New York, NY 10018, USA

E-mail: shire@bloomsbury.com

www.shirebooks.co.uk

SHIRE is a trademark of Osprey Publishing Ltd

First published in Great Britain in 2020

A catalogue record for this book is available from the British Library.

ISBN: PB 978 1 78442 371 1

eBook 978 1 78442 372 8

ePDF 978 1 78442 369 8

XML 978 1 78442 370 4

20 21 22 23 24   10 9 8 7 6 5 4 3 2 1

Typeset by PDQ Digital Media Solutions, Bungay, UK

Printed and bound in India by Replika Press Private Ltd.

Shire Publications supports the Woodland Trust, the UK's leading woodland conservation charity.

MIX
Paper from
responsible sources
FSC
www.fsc.org   FSC® C016779

COVER IMAGE

Front cover: An old railway route and bridge at South Cerney, now a wildlife corridor at Cotswold Water Park that runs between South Cerney and Cricklade. It was once part of the Midland and South Western Junction Railway (David Hall/Alamy). Back cover: A hut on the disused Buchan Railway Line in 2015 (Iain Cameron/CC BY 2.0).

TITLE PAGE IMAGE

A fine semaphore signal (see pages 44–45) with most of its components still in place along the old railway between March and Spalding. This site, now Ring End Nature Reserve, was at the northern end of a once huge goods yards at March, Cambridgeshire, and this signal covered a siding for trains heading south.

CONTENTS PAGE IMAGE

The platforms, stationmaster's house and signal box survive at Stixwould Station, Lincolnshire, along with a rare original name board. The line has now become part of the Water Rail Way.

ACKNOWLEDGEMENTS

All images are from the author's own collection, except for those on the cover.

CONTENTS

A BRIEF HISTORY

RAILWAYS WERE THE wonder of the Victorian age. They transformed long distance travel, aided the growth of industry, encouraged the development of urban areas, and sparked commuting and tourism for the masses. In order for the railways to work efficiently engineers had to design new types of bridges and viaducts, build stations to allow passengers to access trains, and develop signalling and telegraph systems to make sure they arrived safely. Their work was such a success that the rail network grew from a few hundred miles during the 1830s to a peak of around 23,000 miles shortly before the First World War, with the public served by over 10,000 stations. Despite the loss of much of this Victorian network during the second half of the twentieth century, the opening up of many disused lines as footpaths, cycle trails or nature reserves has allowed the public to explore and discover relics of these once mighty railways. Imposing structures, ruined buildings and mysterious posts or platforms can still be found amongst the trees and undergrowth, as this book sets out to describe and explain.

Before tracing lost railways on the ground it is worth looking at documentation, which you can discover from the comfort of your home. Old maps are a rich source of information. Railway companies and private publishers issued many forms of contemporary maps and plans, some of which can be found online, showing the routes of old lines, the location of stations and sometimes even the layout of track and

OPPOSITE
It is hard to believe that express trains from London to Manchester were speeding through Great Longstone Station, Derbyshire, a little over fifty years ago. Today it makes for a tranquil scene enjoyed by walkers and cyclists on the popular Monsal Trail.

Lost railways have been reclaimed by nature and form vital green corridors for wildlife, with trees and flowers enhancing the experience for today's travellers on foot and bike, as here at Midford, near Bath, along the old Somerset and Dorset Railway.

buildings. Ordnance Survey 1 inch to the mile maps and Bartholomew ½ inch to the mile maps published from the 1920s to the 1970s are an even better way of locating lost railways and stations, as they show their relationships to roads, towns and villages. These can still be found in secondhand bookshops on the high street or online, as well as on web-based auction sites. There are also websites holding useful information on the history of a particular railway or site (www.disused-stations.org.uk is a good example).

It is possible to trace the line of old railways by using online satellite imagery. Look for thin lines of greenery gracefully sweeping in wide curves and straight lines across the landscape. These will usually be in the form of a line of trees and scrub unless the railway is now used as a farm track or public path in which case expect to find a double line of hedgerows or fencing coursing across the landscape. Be suspicious if there are very sharp turns, right angles or a T-shaped junction along its route, as these are more likely to be an old canal, drainage channel or road. Where the area of greenery widens or the boundaries spread out it can signify this is an embankment or a cutting. If the line appears to suddenly vanish it could be the site of an old tunnel, especially if there are wide areas of greenery leading up to it. Alternatively it could be a stretch that has been ploughed away although the route of the old railway may still show up as a light or dark line across the soil or a crop mark in a field. Old railway bridges and viaducts will also show up on satellite images as a straight or slightly curving pair of lines with abutments angled away at each end. Look for shadows to the side of these on the photograph: these can sometimes reveal the form of the structure.

In urban areas the route of a railway has often been built upon, making tracing its course trickier. However, the railway would have been sold off to developers in pockets of land that respected the original boundaries; the old route can be followed in a line of new buildings or roads with the occasional undeveloped stretch of greenery or old bridge abutments. Old stations were set upon a wider linear stretch of land – usually with tapered ends – and the boundaries of these can often be seen close to the centre of an urban area. Look out for new industrial units, housing or retail parks in this shape which seem to follow the line of the railway, as these have frequently been built on old stations. Also keep a keen eye out for buildings that are aligned on a different angle to those around them, especially if they seem parallel to the route you are following, as these could be old railway buildings. Victorian terraces and streets often have abrupt straight or angled ends to a row, which can show where a railway once ran.

When looking at maps or satellite images the way in which the old railway cuts across the landscape can tell you something about the type of line it was. The first tramways or plateways had distinctive sharp bends between lengths of curving or straight track as the horses and short wagons they used could negotiate a tight radius. The builders of the early steam railways during the 1830s and 1840s endeavoured to build their lines with gentle sweeping curves and impressive earthworks and viaducts to keep it as straight and level as possible. However, they faced strong objections from wealthy landowners, especially those with interests in the canals and

Old Ordnance Survey and Bartholomew's maps from the first half of the twentieth century are an excellent way to trace lost railways. This excerpt from the latter shows Radstock (Somerset) in the 1920s with numerous railways marked by black lines. Today these have all gone.

A view showing the route of the old railway between Penrith and Keswick (Cumbria), marked by the white arrows. Notice the gentle sweeping line compared with other features like the river, roads and field boundaries.

turnpike trusts, so their course often had to take awkward diversions around or even underneath a country estate.

From the 1860s many new railways were branches built out to serve towns or villages that had so far missed out on the transport revolution or to access factories, docks, mines and quarries. These branch lines were usually built on a budget and served as many sites along the route as possible. As a result they tend to meander through the countryside with tighter curves than on mainlines.

During the nineteenth century the government made little effort to interfere with railway companies, so the network expanded haphazardly with many lines built to block a competitor or to avoid having to use their routes to access a town or city. Do not be surprised to see numerous old lines and sites of stations on maps or satellite images in large urban areas.

One exception to the government's non-interventionist approach was the Light Railways Act of 1896, designed to encourage the building of lines into struggling rural communities. By removing the need for an Act of Parliament and enforcing lower speed and weight restrictions these lines could be built cheaply, taking a winding route up valleys or rattling around fields often with tight curves and steep

James Watt's grandson forced the Grand Junction Railway to run around the edge of Birmingham in order to avoid crossing his estate. This resulted in an awkward arrangement at Curzon Street Station (seen here – a remarkable survival), so a more convenient site at New Street was opened in the 1850s and Curzon Street became a goods depot.

gradients. Even at this late date competition could still be ferocious and a number of mainlines with relatively straight routes, wide sweeping curves and major engineering projects were undertaken: some as shortcuts to improve service; others as a diversionary route to avoid a railway company having to use a competitor's line to access an important city.

Manchester Central Station was just one of a number of major termini in the city but was closed in 1969 when the railways in the area were rationalised. It has since been converted into a concert and exhibition centre.

KEEPING A LEVEL TRACK

T HE ADVANTAGE OF railways over other forms of land transport is that metal wheels running along metal rails can carry heavier loads more smoothly and at greater speed. This is mainly due to the lack of friction between the two surfaces; however, this in turn creates a problem with traction. Railways therefore had to be built on the level or with gentle gradients so trains could operate without excessive slipping – especially in the early days when steam locomotives were not very powerful. Engineers achieved this by constructing viaducts, bridges and embankments to cross valleys, and by creating cuttings and tunnels to go through hills.

The early horse-drawn railways, often referred to as tramways, wagonways or plateways, were generally used to bring coal or stone down from hilly areas to rivers and canals. They wound their way around the contours on a roughly level track and then negotiated hills by using inclined planes. These were steep, even slopes with the trains of wagons let down the track using ropes or chains and the empties pulled back up either by a stationary steam engine or the weight of loaded trains going down. The remains of these inclined planes can still be found today and there are examples with their original stationary steam engine houses on the High Peak Trail along the old Cromford and High Peak Railway. The winding course of these early railways also helped keep major earthworks and engineering structures to a minimum although there are some impressive early examples still in place. The Causey Arch, near

OPPOSITE
Headstone Viaduct, near Bakewell (Derbyshire), is today the highlight of the Monsal Trail but was decried by John Ruskin when built 150 years ago as it destroyed a glorious valley, just so that 'every fool in Buxton can be in Bakewell in half an hour'.

The impressive Hengoed Viaduct at Maesycwmmer in South Wales was built in the 1850s and today carries part of the Celtic Trail cycle route over the Rhymney River. The quarry used to supply the stone and some workers' houses still survive close by.

Stanley, County Durham, is a single span masonry bridge built in around 1726 to carry a wagonway from a nearby colliery. The arch was the widest built at the time and so concerned its builder that he is said to have committed suicide from worry that it would collapse.

As the railway network began to expand from the 1830s with a roughly level track, engineers had to build numerous bridges and viaducts. Some had a simple round arch which transferred the forces exerted upon it vertically down into

This grand railway bridge near Dewsbury, Yorkshire, has very shallow masonry segmental arches. Today it carries the Spen Valley Greenway over the River Calder.

the ground either side, making it strong and easy to calculate for. The problem with this form was that in order to make the span wider you had to make the arch taller, which was usually impractical. A segmental arch, in effect the upper segment of a round arch, created a longer, shallower span, but exerted a horizontal force so required solid ground or strong abutments either side to keep it stable. As a result segmental arches were not always suitable for viaducts where they could push out the tall piers and approaching embankments.

An arch is only stable when all segments are in place, so during construction temporary timber arches called 'centring' were fitted underneath. Projecting stones or sockets which these rested upon can still be seen on the underside of the arches on some viaducts and bridges today. In most cases the masonry used in a bridge came from excavations made during construction

A close-up of a viaduct pier with the carved letter 'A' (a mason's mark). The hole above was made for lifting it into position.

Ham Green Viaduct at Bickleigh, near Plymouth, was built in 1899, partly using blue-grey engineering bricks to replace an old timber structure, the ivy-covered piers of which still stand behind it. Note the projecting stones under the arches, which the centring rested upon.

of the railway or from a local quarry. Working it was a skilled job and if you look on the piers and abutments of bridges and viaducts you can sometimes see carved letters, symbols or shapes left behind to record the work of individual masons. Some blocks will also have a small round depression, which was made so that a stonemason's lewis, a scissor-like pair of tongs, could grip the blocks as they were craned into position.

As the railway network grew, so brick became more popular for arched bridges and viaducts even in areas where stone was readily available. Locally produced bricks were used in the early days, their colour determined by the clays found in the area. In the second half of the nineteenth century more durable mass-produced bricks were being transported around the country for railway projects. Blue-grey engineering bricks, which were very hard and durable, are particularly distinctive of later Victorian railways, and can also be seen where repairs were made to older structures. An alternative to these materials

Stamford Bridge Viaduct, Yorkshire, was built in 1847 with a series of cast-iron arches supporting the railway deck. Notice that the arches rest on angled abutments on the brick piers.

was iron, which could be cast into sections and bolted together to make a large segmental arch. These can look similar to other forms of metal bridge but can be distinguished as the ends rest upon a sloping stone or brick abutment with its face at right angles to that of the arch.

Although masonry and brick arched railway bridges and viaducts continued to be built throughout the nineteenth century, the need for cheaper, lighter and longer spans inspired engineers to experiment with girder bridges. These comprised

Many early railway bridges were made with timber trusses. This old tramway bridge over the River Ribble in Avenham Park, Preston, was rebuilt in concrete to preserve its original form.

Due to mining subsidence the Bennerley Viaduct on the Nottinghamshire and Derbyshire border was built in wrought iron with latticework girder spans. This made a lighter structure than if it had been built in brick.

The Meldon Viaduct, Devon was built in 1874 with wrought iron columns and Warren truss spans. Today it carries the Granite Way over the West Okement River.

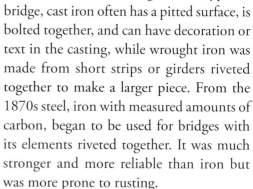

trusses, a framework of struts and posts, which stiffened and supported the deck of the bridge. Some examples were made using timber, usually where other materials would be more expensive or as a short-term solution when money was tight. Cast iron was used on many early railways but its brittle nature soon limited its use to sections under compression like columns and posts. Wrought iron was more expensive but was stronger under tension so could be used in combination with cast iron or on its own. When looking at these types of bridge, cast iron often has a pitted surface, is bolted together, and can have decoration or text in the casting, while wrought iron was made from short strips or girders riveted together to make a larger piece. From the 1870s steel, iron with measured amounts of carbon, began to be used for bridges with its elements riveted together. It was much stronger and more reliable than iron but was more prone to rusting.

The first type of truss that was widely used was the lattice girder, with a regular diagonal grid of metal struts. As confidence grew, more economical types using vertical and diagonal cross members to form triangles

Naburn Swing Bridge near York has two wrought-iron arched plate girder spans, the nearest of which rotated on the huge cylindrical base, which still contains much of the original workings.

(a geometric shape that cannot be distorted) were also developed. Plate girder bridges became popular for shorter spans; these had a simple box framework with flat metal panels riveted across it. Bowstring trusses were also developed, where a large arch helped stiffen a long truss bridge. All these truss or girder bridges were built as self-supporting structures. If you look underneath they should rest upon vertical piers or columns, usually with some form of horizontal pad or rollers between to absorb vibration and expansion. In the 1890s concrete began to be used as a substitute for masonry as it was strong in compression, and by the early twentieth century metal reinforcement was being added to the material to make it strong under tension and hence more flexible. Most railway bridges built since the First World War use steel and concrete in their construction.

An often-overlooked piece of engineering to help a railway maintain

Footbridges could be found linking station platforms or carrying footpaths across the railway. This decorative example spans the Brampton Valley Way in Northampton-shire.

A narrow masonry-lined cutting and bridges through Heckmondwike, Yorkshire, which now forms part of the Spen Valley Ringway.

a level or gentle gradient was the creation of cuttings and embankments. To some extent the two went hand in hand, as the engineer would try to plan the route such that the spoil excavated from cuttings and tunnels would be used to build the neighbouring embankments. Some embankments were carefully constructed in layers, with each compacted before the next was laid upon it. This helped to create a stable bank, but was a slow and complicated process and most railway engineers opted for a faster 'end tipping' process. As a cutting was dug out so rails were laid down from the excavations to the start of the nearest embankment where horses or a locomotive could haul wagons full of the spoil and tip them over the end to build up the embankment. Sometimes it was not possible or economic to balance out the excavated spoil and embanking. Excess material from a cutting could be dumped in a long bank along the top of the works or in spoil heaps nearby, while an embankment could be built up from material dug out of trenches run along each side of the structure. Earthwork embankments and cuttings were set at a determined angle for stability, usually around one and a half

The robust portal to Kelmarsh Tunnel, Northamptonshire, on the Brampton Valley Way.

or two times wider than they were tall. Cuttings could be sheer sided through solid rock or faced with brick and stone through some urban areas where land was valuable.

Tunnels can be the highlight – or perhaps the scariest part – of a journey along an old railway track. There were over a thousand built in Britain for the railway network, nearly half of which are disused. Their form generally reflects the geology faced by the railway builders and the need to hold the ground at bay: the portals and abutments at each end prevented material falling down onto the tracks; the arched lining inside supported the soil and rock above and reduced the amount of water entering; and the vertical shafts provided access during construction and fresh air after it was complete.

Short tunnels had their course laid out across the top of the hill by men lining up a series of sighting poles between each end until a straight route was established. A team at each end could then dig in until they met each other in the middle. Longer tunnels were built using a series of vertical shafts along the planned line of the tunnel, through which men, tools and materials could be lowered and spoil extracted during

The rock-hewn southern portal of Shute Shelve Tunnel, along the Strawberry Line, Somerset.

The inside of a former railway tunnel at Tregarth, Gwynedd, on the Ogwen Trail. The arched recesses were designed for maintenance men to withdraw into when a train passed.

construction. First the shafts were excavated until the correct depth had been reached, then the navvies could start digging out along the horizontal in each direction, creating a narrow tunnel that would establish the centre line when each section met the next. Once this was completed, teams of labourers and bricklayers or stonemasons would start excavating the full-sized tunnel and building the lining. This might be a few bricks thick through good ground but was usually six or eight courses through softer material. The depth of the lining is often exposed around the edge of the opening at the portals.

When complete some of the shafts were left open so they could continue to be used for venting the tunnel. Today the tops of these shafts are useful for spotting the course of an old railway and you can sometimes see the old spoil heaps close by, covered with trees or vegetation, from when the tunnel was built. At over a mile in length, Combe Down Tunnel in Bath is now the longest cycling tunnel in Britain. Unusually it has no air shafts so would have been a horrendous

experience for steam engine drivers. To ease passage for walkers and cyclists today, music and coloured lights have been installed in the centre.

An old air shaft on a tunnel along the Brampton Valley Trail, Northamptonshire.

Railway companies were proud of their tunnels and often lavished the portals with architectural features, especially in the early days. Later ones were usually more functional and some were just hewn from the rock. Inside the tunnel, the base you walk or ride upon is a bed of ballast but underneath was usually an inverted arch, which acted as a foundation for the structure and aided drainage. There might also be pipes or drainage channels along the sides to help carry away excess water and metal hooks or brackets for cables and telegraph wires. Regular checks of the tunnel had to be made, so manholes – small arched recesses in the wall – were provided where workers could rush to when a train passed by. Digging tunnels was the most hazardous aspect of railway construction, with accidents during blasting and collapsing roofs when pockets of shifting sands or gravels were hit claiming most lives. Sometimes the graves of navvies can be found in the church of the parish through which the tunnel was built.

SERVING THE COMMUNITY

RAILWAY STATIONS WERE the communications centres of the community, where passengers could embark on journeys and where telegrams, parcels and letters would be received and sent. At the same time they were the public face of the railway company. In the early days the grand brick or masonry buildings were intended to reassure the public that these thundering, speeding steam engines were safe and that railways were here for the long term. As the network developed, stations were built in the latest architectural styles with lavish accommodation reflecting a company's confidence, ambition and more often than not a desire to outshine a competitor. Stations were constantly being updated and improved and these adaptations can often still be seen when looking at surviving structures today. Changes in the materials used, or parts that differ in style, can indicate a later rebuilding or an extension. Some stations were also added to existing railways at a later date to drive additional traffic onto the trains. Others were originally built on a tight budget or in an inconvenient location so may have been rebuilt, in some cases more than just once.

The main station buildings that can still be found alongside old railways today were designed for a number of roles. The main roadside entrance led into the booking hall in which tickets were purchased, usually with a large doorway to allow for a rush of people exiting trains. To the side of this would have been an office or a suite of them for processing and

OPPOSITE
Nottingham London Road Station dates from the late 1850s and features polychromatic brickwork, steep pitched roofs, prominent chimneys and a crest of railings, which would be fashionable in the following decades. The line was closed to passengers in 1944 but the station remained in use as a mail and parcels depot until the 1970s. The building now serves as a health club.

Clare Station, along the Great Eastern Railway's Stour Valley line in Suffolk, was opened in 1865 with its buildings designed in their standard corporate style. Unusually, the main buildings, platforms, goods shed, a crane, and even station signposts have survived within Clare Castle Country Park.

recording ticket sales, sorting parcels, and receiving telegrams, some also with a separate room for the stationmaster. Stations also had to cater for a social system where divisions in class and sex were rigidly maintained; hence in larger buildings there could be numerous doors leading into separate waiting rooms for men and women, or first and third class. In Victorian

Rayne Station, Essex, was built in 1869 along the Bishop's Stortford to Braintree line and now houses a tearoom for the Flitch Way. The tall central section was the stationmaster's house with the booking hall to the right.

times train journeys were often broken up by having to wait to change trains and as a result some key stations had rooms for refreshments. A house was also provided on site for the stationmaster. This was usually part of the main station building and is recognisable today as the tall two- or three-storey section. Alternatively a separate house was built close by, often sited at the entrance to the station. There may have also been rows of cottages nearby for other members of railway staff. Larger stations, often at the end of a line, may have acted as the headquarters for a local railway company with additional rooms incorporated into their design.

The portico from the Classical style façade of the original Barnard Castle Station, County Durham, was dismantled and moved to Valley Gardens, Saltburn-by-the-Sea, near Middlesbrough, where it remains to this day.

The style of the passenger station buildings not only reflects the ambitions of its builders but also gives a clue as to when it (and in many cases the railway itself) was built. The first stations erected in the 1830s were usually designed in a Classical style. These were inspired by the buildings of the Ancient World and had a simple geometric form, symmetrical façade, the roof hidden behind a parapet and a pediment or portico (a porch on columns) across the doorway. In the following decades the Italianate style was very popular, such that it was often referred to as the 'railway style'. Some were built like grand Italian palaces with symmetrical façades featuring windows surrounded by prominent architraves and pediments, and a bold bracketed cornice and balustrade around the top. More modest stations had a simplified form inspired by Italian country villas with low-pitched roofs

Alton Towers Station, Staffordshire, was completed in 1850 in an Italianate style with an asymmetrically sited tower at the request of the Earl of Shrewsbury, to impress guests at his neighbouring country house. You can still see today where the platforms were extended in concrete to cope with extra tourist traffic after the First World War.

overhanging the walls, paired or triple arched openings, and on some a tower placed asymmetrically along the front. Many smaller stations built in the early days took the form of a simple large house with a shallow pitched slate roof and sash windows divided up by numerous glazing bars.

Whilst these Classical styles still found favour in some quarters, architects and engineers increasingly sought

Hornsea Town Station, Yorkshire, was opened in 1864 with an Italianate façade behind which would have been waiting rooms and offices with the stationmaster's house at the far right end. It now marks the start of the Hornsea Rail Trail and the Trans Pennine Trail.

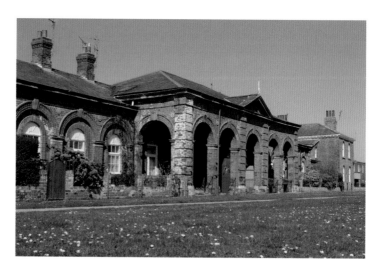

inspiration from Britain's historic past. In the 1840s a revival of Tudor and Elizabethan styles found favour with tall chimneys, shallow pointed arches above doorways, leaded glass in the windows and diagonal patterns in the brickwork. Jacobean-style stations were similar but featured Dutch gables, which had a curved and angled profile. By the 1850s the Gothic Revival, which used medieval churches and abbeys as a source of inspiration, began to influence station design. Buildings were asymmetrical in plan and featured pointed arched windows, steeply pitched roofs and decorative timber bargeboards at the end of the gables. These styles helped make exposed brick walls fashionable again and by the 1860s different colours were being used to make polychromatic patterns across the front. Masonry remained popular but now it often had a rough, textured finish to make it look like it had just been hewn from the quarry. Smooth slates were an economical choice for roofing but by the 1860s clay tiles formed into patterned horizontal bands became more fashionable. Larger sheets of glass were also available so sash windows usually had a single vertical glazing bar and later none at all.

The Gothic-style Axbridge Station, Somerset, with decorative bargeboards, pointed arched doorway and bands of decorative tiles typical of the 1860s. It stood along the Cheddar Valley line, part of which is now the Strawberry Line Path.

In the second half of the nineteenth century it became acceptable to blend one historic period or regional style with details from another to create eclectic styles that were distinctive of a railway line or company. Roof tiles with patterns

The restored timber station building at Hulme End on the former Leek and Manifold Light Railway, which opened in 1904. This building and the adjacent engine shed now provide refreshments and facilities for walkers and cyclists at the end of the Manifold Way.

were still popular in the 1870s, some with iron railings along the crest, but by the following decade plain clay tiles came into fashion. Blue-grey engineering bricks were incorporated into station buildings from around this time, especially in the lower courses where they could help resist damp. In the 1880s the Queen Anne Revival style proved suitable for many of the new suburban and rural stations being built at the time with its stout chimneys, Dutch gables, dormer windows and a white cupola on the roof. In the following decades rustic style buildings inspired by the work of the Arts and Crafts movement found favour with some station designers. They had asymmetrical plans and often featured a wide entrance set back under a low arch, with an upper storey covered in a rough finished render, hanging tiles or mock timber framing. It also became fashionable for the upper sash in the windows to be divided up by glazing bars while the lower part remained clear. The Edwardians revived older Classical styles, most notably the Baroque, with symmetrical façades featuring arched pediments above openings, domes along the roof, and richly carved stone decoration.

Mangotsfield Station, Gloucestershire, was opened in 1869 by the Midland Railway. Today it stands along the Bristol to Bath Railway Path and its triangular plan of platforms has been retained along with the masonry façade in this view.

Even when the old station buildings have all gone you can still find the platforms alongside disused railways. In the earliest stations they were not always provided; passengers were expected to mount the coaches in the same manner as for stagecoaches. By the 1840s platforms had become a standard part of the station, either built as rubble-filled structures with a masonry or brick face, or as open timber structures where weight or costs had to be minimised. Look out for changes in the materials or finish of platforms; these can indicate where they have been widened or extended to cope with an increase in traffic. In most cases platforms were positioned either side of a double track but in some stations built in the late nineteenth century a single island platform sited between the two tracks was fashionable. After the First World War concrete was increasingly used to form platforms either with panels or an open framework.

As stations developed it was quickly appreciated that providing a roof across the platforms was a distinct advantage. Canopies were often provided, either supported on cast-iron columns along the platform or bracketed off the

This huge glass and iron train shed is from Bath Green Park Station, opened in 1870 with the building at the far end designed to complement the Georgian city. It is now part of a supermarket car park.

station building. Where these parts survive today you can often find the name of the foundry where they were cast, and sometimes the coats of arms or emblem of the railway company that commissioned them. These canopies usually had glazed roof sections and a profiled timber valance around the edges, often in a form that was distinctive to a line or company, the pointed dagger board pattern proving a popular choice. Larger stations could have a train shed, a huge glazed arched roof covering platforms and track in one. Although glorious in appearance they could be a maintenance headache so in the late nineteenth century more modest steel and glass canopies set in ridge and furrow patterns were widely adopted.

Even where all traces of the station buildings and platforms have gone it is still possible to find their former location. In most cases there would have been a road or track leading up from the street to the station buildings and these can usually be traced on maps or on the ground. The entrance would have been gated and the stout posts for these gates can be found by the road; sometimes the fencing that flanked the access road also survives. When the railway arrived to serve a town or village it was a major development and in most cases a new road was built to connect them or an existing one was altered to gain access. These were nearly always titled Station Road or Street and they are usually still known as such today, giving a major clue when trying to find their former site. In many cases the station has been built upon with housing or industrial units; however, the new estate might have a name that includes station, railway or a railway company name in the title to record where it once stood. The boundaries of the old station are usually preserved from when the sites were sold off, so look for an elongated rectangular plan often with tapered ends on a map, or old walls and railings on the ground.

Halts were small stations, usually with no more than a platform and sometimes a basic shelter. This reconstructed example is at Stane Street, along the Flitch Way in Essex.

Another clue to the existence of an old station is the presence of hotels, inns and pubs built close by to serve the railway. These can be surprisingly large structures with grand façades, indicating how important the settlement either was or was intended to be by an over-optimistic railway company. They will usually have 'railway' or 'station' in their title. Some have been renamed since the closure of the line but the original title might still be carved in stone or cast in terracotta on the front of the building. They are often worth investigating inside, as some have memorabilia from the old railway within the grounds, or old black-and-white photos of the station on the walls.

THE GOODS YARD

INDUSTRY WAS VITAL to the railways. It had been the driving force behind the development of the first lines and it was often the reason why a railway remained open long after passenger traffic had been withdrawn. The commodities that were carried were principally minerals, especially coal and stone, and industrial or agricultural produce. Most stations had sidings and goods handling facilities where loading took place, usually to the side or a short distance down the line from the passenger platforms. In addition to these goods yards there were a number of large goods stations in major towns, cities and ports. Unfortunately these large plots of land have proved too tempting for developers and most have been built upon. However, odd buildings and features have survived and can be seen isolated within industrial estates or when walking or cycling along a lost railway.

Goods stations or depots were separate from the main passenger stations and were exclusively designed to handle a wide range of goods. These were busy centres of activity, some employing thousands of men with networks of sidings, platforms, warehouses and a large undercover section where packages could be sorted, weighed and loaded. The former Liverpool Street Station in Manchester was converted into a goods depot when the Liverpool and Manchester Railway was extended further into the city centre. The original passenger buildings and warehouse are now part of the Science and Industry Museum. Warehouses were built along the railways

OPPOSITE
This magnificent railway warehouse on the site of the Great Northern Friargate goods depot, Derby, has retained a timber lucarne, which would have covered the crane or hoist used to lift produce up to the top floor.

Horses were widely used in goods yards and stations, so stables would have been a feature in many. This rare example at Withernsea in Yorkshire, now converted into apartments, was built for the hotel that stood next to the station at this seaside resort.

in goods stations and yards, ports or docks. Some stored a wide range of goods while others were built to hold specific produce like fruit, cotton or grain. Some were bonded, where items on which duty was to be paid were securely held. They could range in size from a couple of storeys to four or five high and some had rail access inside with platforms and cranes to unload goods. Warehouses had external hoists at the top; these were mounted onto a timber beam or metal girder so goods could be lifted up to each floor, and were usually covered by a projecting structure called a lucarne. If the goods being lifted were vulnerable to the weather then these could be extended down to cover the whole vertical drop. The remains of the beam and sometimes the lucarne can still be seen on some old warehouses today.

Away from these large urban distribution centres were the local goods yards, each with a goods shed providing a secure, covered space for loading. Early types were built in a variety of designs, some at right angles to the track with small turntables built to provide access. By the 1850s they generally took the familiar form of a rectangular building with the track running through it via a large doorway to one side of the gable end. Wagons and vans were hauled by hand or horse,

A grand goods shed in Ashbourne, Derbyshire, which has an opening to the right through which the railway track entered and two roadside doorways with their canopies intact.

This goods shed in Tetbury, Gloucestershire, was built in 1889 from engineering bricks and has the office on the gable end adjacent to the opening for the track. Since closure in 1965 it has been converted into an arts centre.

as steam locomotives were not allowed in goods sheds. There was a platform and a small crane inside where goods could be transferred from railway wagons to road carts or lorries through a large opening along the side wall. This usually had a large canopy above to protect goods from the rain when unloading. Some had windows on the track side to illuminate the interior but these are often short openings high up in the walls or just glazed sections in the roof, as security was important. A small office where the paperwork was sorted out was usually built onto one of the gable ends and some larger types incorporated a warehouse above.

The versatility and quality of goods sheds means that a remarkable number have survived and are in active use today. They are distinguished by the large doorway set to one side on each gable end and the opening along the roadside wall, sometimes still with its canopy. Some early examples also featured

The old coal drops at Whitedale Station on the Hornsea to Hull railway. The track originally ran over the top and coal was dropped down into the brick bunkers below.

architectural embellishments like fashionable window shapes and decorative details formed in brick or stone to complement the main station buildings. Brunel-designed Tudor-style goods sheds still survive at Yate and Stroud Stations in Gloucestershire. A wonderful large Gothic example stands on the site of the old Southampton Terminus Station and can be viewed from Royal Crescent Drive. A grand stone structure that has retained its canopies can be seen opposite Ashbourne Hospital, Derbyshire, at the southern end of the Tissington Trail. Others could be charmingly simple structures to serve small communities. The old goods shed at Caton, Lancashire, alongside the Lune Cycleway has a simple slate hipped roof and narrow round-arched windows, which suits its modern use as a church. Later examples tend to be more workmanlike, often using engineering bricks around openings and for the plinth.

In addition to the goods shed there may have been short platforms, docks and animal pens where livestock and agricultural produce could be transferred between railway and road. The remains of these can sometimes be found close to the main passenger platforms. Most station yards would have had a coal merchant, with bunkers or drops to store it in, and small huts or offices for carrying out their trade.

At Whitedale Station on the Hornsea Rail Trail the brick coal drops have survived in the small yard alongside the platforms and station house, as well as the base of a small timber goods shed which used to back onto the eastern platform. To check that loads coming in and out of the yard were correct a weighbridge was usually sited near to the entrance. Although originally they were usually made from timber, most were later updated with a large steel plate set in a rectangular pit which contained the mechanism connected to gauges in a small brick or stone hut alongside. Quite a few of the small weighbridge buildings have survived close to the entrance of former station yards but examples with their metal plates are more rare.

The remains of the concrete post and metal arm which formed the loading gauge at Meliden, Denbighshire. Originally an arched bar was suspended from the arm.

In order that wagons and vans were not loaded in a way that would clash with bridges and tunnels a loading gauge was positioned on the track leading into the goods yard. This was an upside down L-shaped frame made from metal, timber or concrete with an arched bar suspended from the arm to indicate a maximum safe height. Loading gauges are rare to find along disused railways but there are examples with concrete posts and metal arms at Meliden on the Prestatyn to Dyserth Way and on the Tissington Trail at Alsop Station.

Cranes were once an essential tool in the goods yard. A simple yard crane could be hinged off a goods shed or warehouse wall while a jib crane had a diagonal mounted arm, the jib, braced back by the stay, both of which were swung off a post. There is a good example at The Old Goods Shed at Clare, Suffolk.

This crane at the former Dyserth Station was originally in the goods yard but has now been moved a short way west to mark the beginning of the trail to Prestatyn.

In the early railway days goods were transferred between rail and canal, as the latter often had better access to certain industrial sites. Transshipment sheds still survive in a few locations, with a similar appearance to goods sheds. There are excellent examples south of Cromford and at Whaley Bridge at either end of the old Cromford and High Peak Railway, part of which is now the High Peak Trail. Even where there are no surviving buildings the remains of a wharf, an arm off the canal, or sidings running alongside the waterway can still be found. At Congleton, Cheshire, the short arm off the Macclesfield Canal still marks the point where goods were transferred onto a siding off what is now the Biddulph Valley Way.

Another industrial structure that can be found along many old railways and tramways are lime kilns. Lime was essential for improving agricultural yields, for making mortar, and for use in the chemical industry. Chalk in the south and east could be easily crushed but elsewhere harder limestone was used which had to be burned to turn it into a more manageable powder form. Blocks were put in kilns at temperatures of around 900–1,000°C so it broke down to form quicklime. Water could then be added to form slaked lime, which was less caustic. Kilns were built alongside railways because they were used not only for transporting the lime but also to deliver the coal required to burn it. Most found today are continuous draw kilns: these had a tall vertical shaft with an arched draw hole and hearth at the base; alternate layers of limestone and coal were built up inside the shaft by pouring them in through a hole at the top. There are numerous examples alongside

The transshipment building at Whaley Bridge, Derbyshire. Goods were transferred from the canal, which ran through the central opening, onto a siding off the Cromford and High Peak Railway through the left arch.

railway walks and trails in the North East, Yorkshire and Derbyshire, and particularly good examples near Millers Dale Station on the Monsal Trail, Derbyshire, one of which has tracks around the top showing where the coal and limestone were dropped in.

The top of the lime kilns west of Millers Dale Station on the Monsal Trail, with a wagon on the tracks spiralling around the (now sealed) openings through which limestone and coal were dropped.

OPERATING A RAILWAY

THE DAY-TO-DAY RUNNING of a railway required many elements to ensure the rolling stock was fit for purpose and that passengers could travel safely. The network at its prime was lined with engine sheds and depots where steam locomotives and carriages could be built, repaired and maintained. There were signal boxes where the complex networks of signalling and points were controlled. Communication was vital to the safe operation of the system and telegraph and later telephone lines ran along the railways to keep all elements of the system connected. When old railways were closed most of this infrastructure was removed, the signal boxes abandoned and old engine sheds demolished or converted to other uses. Despite this seemingly wholesale destruction there are fragments to be found today alongside trails as a reminder of the heyday of railway operation.

Engine sheds were buildings in which steam locomotives could be stored overnight, have their boilers cleaned out and worn parts replaced. These could range from a simple corrugated iron or timber shed for a single engine at the end of a local line up to huge brick and stone structures in the main railway centres. Most were rectangular in form but a number of early examples were round, with sidings radiating from a central turntable. Unlike goods sheds, which had an opening to one side of the gable end, engine sheds had either one central opening, or a series of them, symmetrically across the face. They required lots of light to make maintenance easier

OPPOSITE
A stop and distant signal along the Mawddach Trail at Penmaenpool, near Barmouth.

The little branch line to Malmesbury, Wiltshire, was opened in 1877 and required its own engine shed for the locomotive that ran the limited service along the line. This building is the only part of the station to have survived.

so typically had a row of tall openings down both long sides and glazing in the roof. As steam engines were run inside these buildings, ventilation was essential; they could have raised louvred openings down the length of the roof ridge and circular vents at the tops of gables. Inside the engine sheds there would have been inspection pits below the track, deep enough for a man to stand up and work underneath a locomotive.

In the early days, when there were many regionally based companies with their own rolling stock, engine sheds were numerous. They would have been positioned at junctions, interchanges, at the terminus of a railway or strategically on a long-distance route. In some towns and cities each company entering it would have had their own engine shed; Carlisle, for instance, had seven. As the network expanded and smaller companies were bought out by ever-larger ones the maintenance of rolling stock became concentrated in major engine depots and many of the smaller sheds became obsolete. As a result of their early redundancy there are far fewer engine sheds than goods sheds surviving along disused railways.

Steam engines also required coal and water to operate and bunkers and water towers or tanks would have been positioned at key points around the network. Although finding complete examples is rare, the footings where they stood and the pipe work for water can sometimes be found in old stations and yards. A pair of water tanks with their pipe work still intact

stands hidden in the undergrowth just west of Millers Dale Station on the Monsal Trail. Turntables were provided in many engine depots and goods yards for turning engines around or

The rusting shell of an engine shed lost in woodland beside the trail along the old Derby to Ashby de la Zouch Railway north of Melbourne. Note that the two long inspection pits are still visible on the ground.

A rare water tank for filling steam engines beside the old Midland mainline, now the Monsal Trail, at Millers Dale, Derbyshire.

A concrete post, ladder and fixings from an old signal alongside the Mickleover Railway Walk, near Derby.

to move wagons onto sidings. Most examples have been built upon or are still within active railway property but the remains of their circular pits can occasionally be found – for instance alongside the Tanfield Railway Path, south-east of Marley Hill, County Durham, and at Maud Junction, Aberdeenshire, on the Formartine and Buchan Way.

Travellers on the first railways had every right to be frightened, not just because they were travelling at speeds in excess of 30 miles per hour but also because there was little in the way of safety to prevent them crashing. The best that the railway companies offered was to position men with flags so they could warn an oncoming train if another had passed by within the previous ten minutes. The first improvement was to introduce semaphore signals, a tall vertical post with a pivoted indicator arm at the top to show if a line was clear. By the 1870s most had adopted a similar form with a red arm featuring a vertical white stripe, which indicated 'stop' when horizontal and 'all clear' when it was angled up or down. At the opposite end of the arm were red and green lenses (blue glass was used, as it glowed green when in front of the yellow flame of an oil lamp), which gave a corresponding signal at night when they passed in front of a lamp fixed to the post.

As speeds increased it was found that there was not enough time for a train to halt before passing a stop signal. In response distant signals were introduced which gave the driver advanced warning. At first these had red arms like the stop signals but were distinguished by having a 'V' shape cut out of the end, but in the 1920s they were changed to a distinctive yellow with a black chevron. Where there were points and junctions, then a series of signals could be fixed together off a single post or mounted on a gantry. The highest post would usually indicate the main or busiest line and the shorter ones sidings and branches. There were also subsidiary signals, smaller semaphores or ground-mounted pivoting discs, which were typically used to control shunting in sidings. Occasionally signals have been retained along trails, although they may not be in their original location. Some have their red stop or yellow distant arms still in place; in other cases just the post or stump of the signal have survived buried in the undergrowth alongside the path.

A short metal post and pulley through which the cables ran from a signal box to the signals.

Semaphore signals and the points that switched a train from one track to another were initially operated by levers close to each apparatus. As lines became busier from the 1860s, so signal boxes were introduced from which signals and points along a section of the railway could be operated remotely. These distinctive buildings usually had a brick, stone or timber lower storey and a wooden-framed upper section, glazed on three or all sides, to give the signalman a

Electric signals replaced old semaphores during the twentieth century. This example on the left alongside the Spen Valley Greenway, near Dewsbury, has survived minus its lights.

good view. The row of levers controlled by the signalman were pivoted below the floor in a frame within the locking room which occupied the lower section of the signal box. The levers that controlled the points were usually painted black and were connected to them via rods with blue levers used to lock them in position. Levers to control signals were red and yellow to correspond with stop and distant types and were connected via wires. The wires and rods to the signals and points ran out through a slot underneath the signal box. Where the signal box was sited at the station itself then the opening was usually at the bottom of the face of the platform and these gaps can often be seen today. At Hadlow Road Station, in The Wirral, there is a shallow arched opening where the rods and wires ran out from the original signal box on the platform. The restored example which stands there today does not correspond to this

opening, however, as it came from a different station and was set up closer to the station building tearooms.

There were over 10,000 signal boxes at the peak of the railway era but now they can be counted in hundreds with many of these inaccessible on active railways or within private residences. Some excellent restored examples can be seen alongside trails including at Warmley (Bristol), Hartington (Derbyshire), and at Penmaenpool (Gwynedd) on the Mawddach Trail, which has been converted into an observation centre for the Royal Society for the Protection of Birds.

If the railways revolutionised transport in the nineteenth century then the telegraph had the same effect for communication. It enabled a short message to be sent over long distances as a series of electrical pulses down a wire to a receiver at the other end. It proved to be a vital tool for railway

Penmaenpool signal box along the Mawddach Trail has been restored and now serves as an RSPB viewing point for watching birds along this beautiful estuary.

The restored signal box at Warmley, Gloucestershire, along the Bristol and Bath Railway Path.

safety as well as instantaneous messaging for industry and the public. The first commercially successful system was patented by Charles Wheatstone and William Fothergill Cooke in 1837 and a few years later was installed along part of the Great Western Railway. Around the same time in America, Samuel Finley Breese Morse was working on a cheaper telegraph system, which used his Morse code and would be more widely adopted in the long term. Wires and posts spread rapidly along the rail network as it saved the telegraph companies from having to pay numerous landowners charges for crossing their property. At the same time railways benefited as they could use the lines for their own messaging; for instance, signal boxes could send a bell code to the next one along to confirm a train had passed. Telegraph offices were established in most stations so the public or businesses could send messages. They remained useful until the middle of the twentieth century despite the introduction of telephones.

A rare railway telegraph post with numerous arms still intact with their insulators, east of Millers Dale Station along the Monsal Trail.

The wires were supported on tall posts, usually made from larch or pine and coated in creosote. Rows of earthenware, ceramic or glass insulators were positioned along the arms at the top around which the lengths of wires were wound and joined. You can often find the white ceramic insulators on brackets where wires passed along the inside of bridges and tunnels, or on the front of railway stations where the lines entered the building. The posts, which were once a common sight, were generally removed when lines fell into disuse but a few have survived along the side of railway trails if you look in the trees and undergrowth. An excellent example can be found east of Millers Dale Station on the Monsal Trail, which seems to have been preserved as it was later used for mounting an aerial for the hamlet in the valley below. A row of rare metal telegraph posts runs alongside part of the Mawddach Trail near Barmouth.

TRACK AND TRACKSIDE FURNITURE

A WAY FROM THE sites of old stations and goods yards are miles of tranquil tree-lined paths and trails, which seem far removed from the noise and steam of the railway age. Yet even along these greenways there are pieces of railway archaeology waiting to be discovered. Old level crossings, platelayers' huts, signs, fencing and gates still survive hidden in the undergrowth. Even the old railway track is sometimes found while rails and sleepers can be seen reused as fence posts.

The permanent way is the track, ballast and base upon which the trains ran. The track comprised a pair of rails and a row of sleepers, some with metal chairs, a socket which linked the former to the latter. Some of the earliest rails had an L-shaped profile and were mounted on stone blocks so the horses could walk up between them without damaging the track. Edge rails, where the wheel has a flange to keep it within the tracks, became standard by the time the railway network developed in the 1830s. When trains passed along a length of rail the upper part was compressed and the lower was stretched, so engineers made the top and bottom thicker to help resist these forces, hence the familiar profile of rails. Double-headed rails had a symmetrical profile with a thick top and bottom fixed in metal chairs, while flat-bottomed rail had a wide flanged base that could be fixed directly to the sleepers. Bridge rails had an inverted U-shaped profile with flanges sticking out either side of the base for fixing to longitudinal timbers running the length of the rails.

OPPOSITE
An ornate level crossing cottage at Oakamoor, Staffordshire, opposite the start of the Churnet Valley Trail, beautifully restored as a private residence. This style of decorative timber framing above stone or brick was popular during the Victorian period but especially in the 1840s and '50s.

ABOVE LEFT
Old bridge rail, as shown in this example from Somerset, was often reused for fence posts along old Great Western Railway lines.

ABOVE RIGHT
A section of flat-bottomed rail now used as a fence post with the two holes where the fishplates were bolted.

Double-headed rails evolved into bullhead types, which by the late nineteenth century became the standard for most lines. After the Second World War flat-bottomed rails were reintroduced on mainlines and became the preferred choice such that bullhead rails are now usually found only on minor lines, sidings or heritage railways.

Old rails can sometimes still be found trapped in tarmac on old level crossings or left abandoned in undergrowth. It is also common to see lengths of it reused alongside modern trails especially for fence posts. It should be a thick piece of rusty metal around 120–180mm high, a little less on some old narrow-gauge track, often with two or three holes at one end where the fishplates, which held the lengths together, were bolted. Sleepers holding the rails together at the standard gauge of 4ft 8½in (less on narrow gauge railways) were usually made of softwood and treated with creosote or similar preservatives, hence their dark colour. They should have the bolt holes and

Old railway sleepers alongside this Lincolnshire trail set up as fence posts with the addition of angled metal caps. Sleepers usually have distinctive rectangular depressions with three holes, marking where the chair was bolted.

square impression on their upper surface where the chairs holding the rails were fixed. Some can be found stuck in the ground where they were left; others have been used as fence posts and to form seats or steps.

Buffers were positioned at the end of lines and sidings to prevent trains slipping off the end, as with this example made from old rails.

A gradient post along the Tissington Trail showing the incline of 1 in 260 to the right and a much steeper climb of 1 in 59 to the left. Examples of short concrete posts with two holes in the head can often be found alongside some trails; these are gradient posts that have lost their arms.

Ballast was another important part of the permanent way. It helped spread the load and absorb the movement of a train, acted to stop the track drifting out of position and allowed water to drain away. It could be made from locally supplied stone, gravel or industrial by-products although granite was widely used in the twentieth century. Ballast was left in a rough finish so the stones locked together better to prevent it drifting away. Although much of it was usually removed when railways were closed some inevitably remained behind and can be found in patches or scattered along trails today.

A large number of signs and posts were installed along railways to warn train drivers of potential hazards. Unfortunately most were recycled when a line closed or have since been removed by collectors. Amongst the few types that can still be found in situ are gradient posts. Although old railways appear fairly level when walking or cycling along them, most have stretches running up or down a slope and in the days of steam it was important that the driver was aware that they were approaching a steep climb or descent. Gradient posts were sited along the side of the track with arms indicating if they were approaching a climb, descent or a level stretch. On these were written the angle of the incline typically in the form of 1:200, so for every 200 feet travelled the railway climbs or descends 1 foot, with the smaller the second number the steeper the slope. When the railway was flat then the word 'level', L or ∞ was used.

Mileage markers with a single number or fraction on an arched post or angled block can also be found in the undergrowth alongside some trails. Another type of sign was a short metal post with the initials of the railway company

cast on it to mark the boundary of their property. Bridges were numbered to help staff identify a site for maintenance or in an emergency. Look out for numbers painted on the abutments or a geometric impression in the masonry or holes in brickwork where a metal number plate was originally fixed.

The permanent way needed constant checking and maintenance to ensure the safe passage of trains. Platelayers, a title derived from the early plateways, were usually stationed along a section of line to check the condition of the track and infrastructure and carry out any necessary maintenance or repairs. The narrow space alongside the outside edge of the ballast known as the 'cess' was a level path for them to walk along. As they worked very long hours platelayers' huts were provided beside the railway where they could store tools, shelter and sit down for a drink or meal. These huts – made from brick, stone, concrete, timber or steel – can still be found, although sometimes only the footings survive in the undergrowth. They usually had a single sloping or double pitched roof, a window and door and a chimney for a small fireplace or stove inside.

ABOVE LEFT
Mileage posts had to be provided every quarter mile along railways, many with the numbers set on an angle, as in this concrete example, so they would be easier to read from passing trains.

ABOVE RIGHT
Small marker posts were used to delineate a railway company's boundary, as in this Midland Railway example.

Look out for bridge numbers painted on the abutments, as in this example in Lancaster.

It was usually a legal requirement established in the act of Parliament for each railway that the line should be fenced off. As well as marking a railway company's property they also helped keep livestock and trespassers off the track. Timber posts with a number of wire strands was the most common solution on most lines. Many of these were later replaced with concrete or steel posts with metal fixings on the sides, which could have ratchets to tighten the tension in the wire. It is also common for old sleepers and rail to be used as posts.

At the point where busy roads passed over the railway at the same height a level crossing was built. This consisted of a single or paired gate either side of the tracks, which would be used to close off the railway or road. Level crossings were operated by a crossing keeper and as he was usually required most days of the week a cottage was provided next to the crossing. Originally the gates were left across the railway but as train traffic and speeds increased in the early 1840s they were generally left shut across the road. The gates were originally plain but by the 1890s the familiar white timber frames with a large red disc in the centre became standard. It was not until the 1960s when road traffic was growing and there were problems finding reliable keepers that automatic barriers began to be installed.

On most old railways the gates have long since gone, although a few have been restored or had replicas fitted. The timber or concrete posts on which they swung can more frequently be found, sometimes with the metal pintles, the brackets on which the gates swung, still set in them. Even where all traces of the gates have gone the crossing keeper's cottage often survives, usually now a private residence, on the same alignment as the track. The other feature to look out for where you suspect an old railway once crossed a road is a distinctive rise and fall in the road surface. The permanent way was normally slightly higher compared with the approaching road and this change in level can often still be seen even after the road has been resurfaced.

These wonderful relics of our once great railway network should not be taken for granted. The fact we can still explore huge viaducts, dark tunnels and ruined stations is only thanks to the efforts of countless individuals, groups and forward thinking authorities who appreciated their value when others threatened

to swing the demolition ball. In the wake of Dr Beeching's overzealous attempt to streamline the railways, over 6,000 miles of track and 2,000 stations were closed, leaving many

A brick platelayers' hut with chimney and an old gradient post repositioned next to it. Judging by the use of engineering bricks this would date from the late nineteenth century.

Small hoppers were positioned alongside the track, as with this concrete example, to hold spare ballast for platelayers when making daily repairs to the permanent way.

Original concrete railway fencing along the Manifold Way, Staffordshire, dating from the early twentieth century.

once proud railways, the hub of a community, in danger of being forgotten. That which was not redeveloped or ploughed away was rapidly reclaimed by nature and within a few decades shrubs, bushes and trees covered the old embankments and cuttings forming a corridor for wildlife where once steam engines thundered. Yet even as Beeching was wielding his axe preservation groups were being established, at first to prevent the wholesale loss of a line and then slowly to reopen stretches as heritage railways. By the 1980s issues with congestion encouraged groups like Sustrans to campaign for safe routes for cyclists and along with the help of local councils old railways began to be converted into cycle tracks and footpaths. Today old Victorian railway structures and buildings which were once seen as dirty and ugly are being listed and restored as cafés and shops. Yet despite this change in attitude towards our old railways there are many parts in danger of being lost for ever. Old stations are still being built upon and trackside features are continuing to fall into disrepair. Without continuing efforts to recognise their value and save these fragments of our transport heritage many communities will lose these vital links with their past.

PLACES TO VISIT

RECOMMENDED RAILWAY TRAILS

Bath and Bristol Railway Path: A fantastic tarmac route between the cities with numerous railway features including the restored Warmley Station and the ruins of the junction at Mangotsfield.

Brampton Valley Way: Follows the old line between Northampton and Market Harborough. Highlights include two tunnels, an old footbridge, station platforms and a restored stretch of the line now known as the Northampton and Lamport Railway.

Camel Trail: Follows old railways between Padstow and Wenford Bridge via Wadebridge. Beautiful Cornish scenery and the impressive girder bridge over Little Petherick Creek.

Cinder Track or Scarborough to Whitby Rail Trail: A spectacular coastal cycle and walking path passing through the North York Moors National Park. There are old stations and stunning views from Larpool Viaduct over the River Esk.

Downs Link: A long-distance bridleway created on two old railways between Guildford (Surrey) and Shoreham (Sussex). Attractive rolling countryside and old stations at Bramley and West Grinstead.

Flitch Way: Along the route of the former Great Eastern Railway between Bishop's Stortford and Braintree, Essex. The restored stations at Rayne and Stane Street Halt are of note.

Formartine and Buchan Way: Between Dyce, north of Aberdeen, to Maud Junction and then either to Fraserburgh or Peterhead. Long-distance route through Aberdeenshire countryside with much to see including Ellon Viaduct with a telegraph post still fixed to the stonework and Maud Junction with its platforms, buildings and a rare turntable base.

High Peak Trail: From Parsley Hay on the Tissington Trail to High Peak Junction near Cromford. This follows the line of the old Cromford and High Peak Railway with original railway transshipment buildings at Cromford, a number of inclined planes and a restored steam engine at Middleton Top.

Hornsea Rail Trail: From Hornsea on the Yorkshire coast to Hull with numerous old stations along the route culminating in the fine buildings at the seaside resort.

Lune Cycleways: From Canton to Lancaster, including stations, bridges and a chapel in an old goods shed.

Lydgetts Junction, Consett, County Durham: From this old railway junction there are four separate trails following parts of old railways: Consett to Sunderland Cycle Path, Waskerley Way, Lanchester Railway Valley Walk and Derwent Walk Railway Path. Also close by is Causey Arch, the oldest standing railway arched bridge.

Marriott's Way: From Norwich to Reepham along the disused line between the city and Melton Constable. The trail includes girder bridges, station buildings, level crossing gates, and the restored Whitwell and Reepham Station.

Mawddach Trail: A beautiful route along the old railway between Dolgellau and Morfa Mawddach with a signal box, signal and station building at Penmaenpool and iron telegraph posts and a platelayers' hut further along the route. At the western end you can carry on alongside the current line into Barmouth via one of the longest timber railway bridges in the country.

Monsal Trail: From Bakewell to Wyedale near Buxton, Derbyshire. Stunning old line through the heart of the Peak District with five tunnels, numerous viaducts and lots of old railway features to look out for, especially around Millers Dale Station.

National Cycle Network Route 1: Along the old Great North
   of Scotland Railway between Garmouth and Cullen.
   A fragmented route on and off the old line but includes
   spectacular coastal scenery, the huge Spey Viaduct and
   a dramatic entrance to Cullen high above the sea. There
   is also an old timber station building further along the
   line at Portsoy.

National Cycle Network Route 887: Along the old Rhondda
   and Swansea Bay Railway, between Aberavon and
   Blaengwynfi, is a dramatic route up the wooded River
   Afan valley with viaducts at Pontrhydyfen and Cymmer.
   There are ambitious plans to open the 2-mile-long
   Rhondda Tunnel at the northern end of the trail to
   cyclists and walkers.

The Ogwen Trail: From Bangor to Bethesda, North Wales,
   this trail mostly follows the old lines that brought slate
   down from the Welsh mountains and includes bridges,
   a tunnel and a viaduct as well as attractive scenery.

Prestatyn–Dyserth Way: A short route between the two towns
   with a restored goods shed and loading gauge at Meliden
   and a crane at the end of the trail in Dyserth.

Spen Valley Greenway and Spen Valley Ringway: Dewsbury
   to Low Moor near Bradford, and Heckmondwike, West
   Yorkshire. These routes have many old bridges, signals
   and inventive sculptures on the route.

Tarka Trail: Between Braunton and Meeth in Devon is a
   very attractive 30-mile stretch suitable for cycling and
   walking, which follows old lines and features numerous
   relics from the railway age.

Tissington Trail: From Ashbourne to Hurdlow, south of
   Buxton, Derbyshire. Another rewarding route crossing
   limestone country with old stations and railway
   memorabilia hidden along the way.

Two Tunnels Greenway: A dramatic route along the northern
   section of the Somerset and Dorset Railway including

the longest tunnel for walking or cycling in the country
featuring a sound and light display in the centre.

Water Rail Way: Following part of the old railway between
Lincoln and Boston. The route follows the River Witham
and includes a number of old station buildings and a
heritage centre at Bardney.

The Wirral Way: Along the former railway between West
Kirby and Hooton. This line runs along the Dee Estuary
and through the Wirral Country Park before turning
inland and passing through the attractively restored
Hadlow Road Station.

HERITAGE RAILWAYS WITH ORIGINAL BUILDINGS AND RAILWAY INFRASTRUCTURE

Bluebell Railway, Sheffield Park Station, East Sussex
TN22 3QL. Telephone: 01825 720800.
Website: www.bluebell-railway.com

Bo'ness and Kinneil Railway, Union Street, Bo'ness, Falkirk
EH51 9AQ. Telephone: 01506 822298.
Website: www.bkrailway.co.uk

Churnet Valley Railway, Kingsley and Froghall Station,
Froghall, Staffordshire ST10 2HA. Telephone: 01538
750755. Website: www.churnetvalleyrailway.co.uk

East Lancashire Railway, Bolton Street Station, Bury,
Lancashire BL9 0EY. Telephone: 0333 320 2830.
Website: www.eastlancsrailway.org.uk

Gloucestershire Warwickshire Steam Railway, The Railway
Station, Toddington, Gloucestershire GL54 5DT.
Telephone: 01242 621405. Website: www.gwsr.com

Great Central Railway, Loughborough Central Station,
Loughborough LE11 1RW. Telephone: 01509 632323.
Website: www.gcrailway.co.uk

Keighley and Worth Valley Railway, The Railway Station, Haworth, West Yorkshire BD22 8NJ. Telephone: 01535 645214. Website: www.kwvr.co.uk

Kent and East Sussex Railway, Tenterden Town Station, Tenterden, Kent TN30 6HE. Telephone: 01580 765155. Website: www.kesr.org.uk

Llangollen Railway, The Station, Abbey Road, Llangollen LL20 8SN. Telephone: 01978 860979. Website: www.llangollen-railway.co.uk

Mid Hants Railway, Station Road, New Alresford, Hampshire SO24 9JG. Telephone: 01962 733 810. Website: www.watercressline.co.uk

Nene Valley Railway, Wansford Station, Stibbington, Peterborough PE8 6LR. Telephone: 01780 784444. Website: www.nvr.org.uk

North Norfolk Railway, Station Approach, Sheringham, Norfolk NR26 8RA. Telephone: 01263 820800. Website: www.nnrailway.co.uk

North Yorkshire Moors Railway, Park Street, Pickering, North Yorkshire YO18 7AJ. Telephone: 01751 472508. Website: www.nymr.co.uk

Severn Valley Railway, Comberton Place, Kidderminster, Worcestershire DY10 1QR. Telephone: 01562 757900. Website: www.svr.co.uk

South Devon Railway, Dartbridge Road, Buckfastleigh, Devon TQ11 0DZ. Telephone: 01364 644 370. Website: www.southdevonrailway.co.uk

Swanage Railway, Station House, Swanage, Dorset BH19 1HB. Telephone: 01929 425800. Website: www.swanagerailway.co.uk

West Somerset Railway, The Railway Station, Minehead, Somerset TA24 5BG. Telephone: 01643 704996. Website: www.west-somerset-railway.co.uk

INDEX